THE BARTENDER'S GUIDE TO
GIN

THE BARTENDER'S GUIDE TO

GIN

Classic and Modern-day cocktails for gin lovers

LOVE FOOD™

CONTENTS

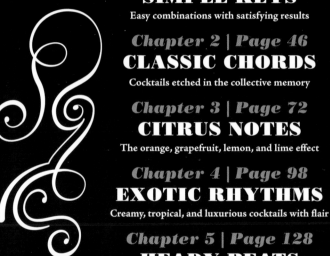

A brief
HISTORY
of GIN

The gin we know today tells a story that spans many centuries. From its most humble beginnings as a drink of the poor and destitute to its association as the drink of privilege and royalty, gin has an especially colorful tale to tell.

Distillation, of which gin is just one product, is an ancient art—the first stills were filled by Arabic alchemists in the Far East as early as the first century, when the Roman Empire was in full swing and Christianity was in its formative years. These early scientists spent decades distilling all kinds of elixirs, gleaning knowledge from other specialists of the time, such as the Greeks.

By the twelfth century, the knowledge had been absorbed into Europe and was being used by Benedictine monks in Salerno, Italy. At this point, spirit was being used for medical

and scientific reasons to preserve the rare and precious ingredients used in medicine. These early distillations of alcoholic spirit would have tasted truly awful, due to the primitive distillation process.

Thanks to the Benedictine monks, distillation began to spread gradually through other monasteries in Europe. The process was still crude, but over the centuries it was refined by Europe's scientific minds. By the 1600s, distillation was widely practiced, and the use of grain- and grape-based spirits was commercialized into liquors, such as Chartreuse, Armagnac brandy, and gin's forerunner, genever.

Genever is a grain-based spirit made in pot stills, (much like whiskey), flavored with juniper and in some cases aged in oak casks. The name "genever" is derived from the Dutch word for juniper and is pronounced *yeh-nih-ver*. It is still made in some of the oldest distilleries in the world, such as Amsterdam's Bols Distillery, which dates back to 1575. Nowadays, genever isn't so well known outside the Low Countries and specialty drinks circles, but without it we would not have gin as we know it.

Gin became hugely popular throughout the 1600s. The Thirty Years' War, which raged across Europe from 1618 until 1648, made other alcohol much harder to acquire, while the Dutch East India Trading Company (known as the VOC) was actively developing overseas markets. Genever had also become a staple of the Dutch military and, in turn, of English soldiers who had been sent by Queen Elizabeth I to fight alongside them. The Thirty Years' War was one of Europe's bloodiest wars, but we do have it to thank for the dramatic influx of genever coming across the English Channel.

The taste for gin soon became ingrained in London. In the early 1700s, British distillers eager to emulate the flavor and success of genever started to produce the first English gin. Because there were no strict laws surrounding licensing and production, London hosted a huge boom in alcohol. These early English gins were made using various methods and ingredients; some were downright toxic, but they were all made from grain and flavored with juniper. The period from the early 1700s to the 1750s is the ugliest chapter in gin's history—and the source of many of the myths that still surround the liquor. After a series of acts introduced by the government to control the gin craze, London started to sober up and some iconic gin brands began to emerge.

With the 1800s came the age of the cocktail, and in the 1830s the birth of the "column still", which was to revolutionize the production of gin, and all spirits. The column enabled a far purer spirit style because of its vastly more efficient distillation mechanics. With a cleaner and purer spirit, producers started to remove the sugar and other additives, which were no longer needed to mask their distillates—and dry gin was born.

Illustration of a gin shop from Charles Dickens' *Sketches by Boz* (1836)

English Gin was now on the up, the hideous gins of the 1700s had gone, and fine-quality dry gins began to be enjoyed the world over. The drink flourished even during U.S. Prohibition, and after surviving two world wars, it bounced back and continued to grow into the mid-1950s. Gin then took a back seat, making way for vodka, but from the 2000s onward we have seen a true renaissance, and an explosion of gins being produced around the world.

FROM GRAIN *to* GLASS

In its simplest form, gin is a pure spirit that has been flavored with juniper and other botanicals. A spirit is generally made using either pot or column stills and is the product of distilling an alcoholic solution that is usually made from grapes or grains.

The majority of gins start life as a neutral grain spirit (NGS). This spirit is the product of column distillation, a technique that has been practiced since the mid-1800s. It has revolutionized the production of alcohol and is used on a mammoth scale in huge distilleries, some of which are capable of producing in excess of 26-million gallons of pure alcohol per annum.

These distilleries are essential to the whole alcohol industry, despite being a far cry from the shiny copper stills used in the final stages of the original process of making gin. To understand NGS and how it is used to make gin, you first need to have an understanding of exactly how alcohol is made.

All alcoholic drinks are the product of a serendipitous relationship between yeast and sugar. Yeast is a single-cell organism and a fungus that, given the right conditions, can transform the fermentable sugars in a sugary liquid into alcohol. The origin of the base liquid will determine the type of beverage that is being made, so grape juice makes wine, apple juice makes hard cider, and malt-based liquids make beer.

The art of fermentation has been practiced for thousands of years and has now evolved into the many alcoholic beverages we see today.

The spirit used to make the vast majority of English gins is made from grain and distilled using column stills. The grain is milled, mashed with hot water, and fermented with yeast to create what the alcohol industry calls "wash." The distillation of liquor works under the basic principle that alcohol has a lower boiling temperature than water. As heat is applied to the still and the temperature rises, the alcohol will begin to separate from the wash and rise up the still as a vapor; it is then collected and condensed back into a liquid, creating the spirit. Column stills are incredibly efficient and, unlike other types of stills, they can produce an immaculate distillate of incredibly high strength, removing nearly all the impurities along the way. This makes it perfect for making gin.

Unlike malt whiskey or Cognac brandy distilleries, many gin distillers tend not to start with the raw materials and fermentation, instead buying NGS and redistilling, rectifying, and tweaking it to meet their requirements. This has been encouraged by EU laws on the production of Dry and London gins, dictating that a neutral spirit of no less than 96 percent alcohol by volume (ABV) must be used as the base spirit for distilled and London/Dry gin. Achieving these strengths with more traditional distilling setups can be difficult. The resulting base spirit is then combined with botanicals to produce the flavor.

Distillers use various methods, equipment, and types of stills to infuse and entwine their botanicals into their liquor. The quantities and combinations of botanicals used, along with the infusion methods and equipment used, dictate the gin's style and flavor.

The two most common methods are the "steep-and-boil" method and "vapor infusion" method.

Steep and boil, as the name suggests, involves steeping the botanicals in a base spirit that has been cut down to 50–60 percent abv. Some producers leave the botanicals for a couple of days, others for just a few hours. The next step involves distilling the spirit once again, which finishes the infusion of the botanicals into the spirit.

A gin bottling plant.

For vapor-infused gins, the botanicals are suspended in a basket, usually in the neck of the still—the spirit vapor collects the oils and flavors as it is forced through the basket. Once the vapor has cooled and condensed, a flavorful gin emerges.

Other methods are used, but the goal is always to infuse the botanicals into the spirit. Regardless of the exact distillation and infusion methods, all gins are finally cut down with water to a bottling strength, in most cases 37.5 percent abv. This is the legal minimum, but less water can be used, resulting in a stronger release.

BOTANICALS

Botanicals are to gin what paint is to a canvas—without them, gin would simply be a neutral liquor with no character. Under the watchful eye of a gin distiller, the botanicals will relinquish their precious oils into the liquor, creating a kaleidoscope of flavors.

By far the most important botanical is juniper. It is, by law, the dominant flavor in gin and provides the lion's share of aroma. Its cones, better known as berries, are bold and fragrant with oil-rich seeds, providing the precious compounds that create the gin's signature flavor. The chemical compound alpha-pinene is dominant, contributing pine, rosemary, lavender, heather, and camphor flavors, to name just a few. It also contains limonene, which adds citrus flavors. Both of these compounds appear in many of the botanicals used in the making of gin and are found throughout the plant world, designed to deter hungry insects. It just so happens that what insects don't like, gin drinkers do.

Juniper

Juniper is a robust plant that grows all around the world, but in the making of gin it is mainly sourced from Eastern Europe, Tuscany, and Morocco. The plant is difficult and time-consuming to harvest, because each plant bears both ripe and unripe berries all year round. On top of this, each berry can take three years to mature before finally being ready to pick. This means the berries must be collected by hand to avoid disturbing the ripening berries and the following year's crop. Every year, hundreds of tons of juniper berries will be harvested from the wild, destined for the production of gin.

Juniper plays its part in the flavoring of gin alongside other botanicals, just like the instruments in an orchestra, to create a symphony of flavor. The most common botanicals found in gin, aside from juniper, are coriander seeds, angelica root, orris root, cassia bark, licorice, and citrus peel.

Coriander seeds

Found in Morocco, Bulgaria, Russia, and Romania, coriander is the second most important botanical—its seeds are rich in the essential oil linalool. It is spicy and aromatic, lending woody notes and sparkling citrus and floral flavors.

Angelica root

Mainly sourced from Germany and Belgium, angelica root shares two of the key compounds found in juniper: the woody alpha-pinene and the citric lemolene, but the overall punch is much softer. The root acts as a bond, helping to tie the more volatile flavors together in the liquor.

Orris root

Among the rarest ingredients used in gin, orris root is often sourced from Florence, Italy. It takes years for the bulbous root to develop in the plant, and it then needs to be stored and dried for another three years. At this stage, the root is hard and needs to be ground into a powder before being used. Its flavor is far less pronounced than juniper and coriander, but it still plays a key role. Like angelica, it helps to fix the more volatile flavor compounds within the liquor. Many gin distillers praise it for its subtlety and perfumed qualities.

Cassia bark

The cassia tree is a member of the cinnamon family and is usually found growing in China, Vietnam, and Madagascar. The bark is collected and dried. Like cinnamon, it brings a warming, festive spiciness.

Licorice root

Found in Indochina, this hard, fibrous root needs to be ground down before use and helps add sweetness and balance alongside the livelier and punchier botanicals.

Citrus peel

Both lemon and orange have a key role in most gins—the peels are stripped from the fruit, bringing in their signature flavors. Oranges and lemons from Seville, Spain, where the peels are removed by hand and left to dry in the sun, are generally favored.

These core botanicals are often supplemented by a medley of others, including cardamom, grains of paradise (alligator pepper), ginger, cubeb berries, and aniseed. Gin producers will often also seek out locally grown botanicals to add unique supporting flavors; these add terroir and provenance to individual gins.

Some of gin's botanical flavorings

With so many exotic, flavorful botanicals, infinite combinations, and multiple infusion methods, gin looks set to continue on its streamlined path of innovation, diversity, and intoxicating flavors.

DEFINITION and STYLES of GIN

Defining "gin"

The legal definition of "gin" is of a distilled liquor that obtains its flavor through juniper and other botanicals. These botanical flavorings can influence the spirit before, during, and after distillation, depending on the production method used.

Gin is produced globally and legal definitions can vary slightly around the world, but the core principals remain the same. The principals are that gin must be distilled from a neutral spirit base of ethyl alcohol and the dominant flavor must be juniper.

The minimum bottling strength for gin in Europe is 37.5 percent ABV, whereas in the United States it is 40 percent ABV, or 80 percent proof. All types of gin made in Europe are bound by the EU Spirit Drink Regulations of 2008, and fall into one of three categories: Gin, Distilled Gin, and London Gin.

Gin

This most basic form of gin is made by adding natural or artificial flavors to the neutral base spirit. This type of gin does not need to be redistilled, and approved artificial colorings and sweeteners can be added. This style is cheaper and easier to make and is usually deemed inferior, due to the lack of restrictions surrounding the quantities of the additives used.

Distilled Gin

This type of gin is made by redistilling a neutral base spirit of at least 96 percent ABV in the company of botanicals. The resulting flavor-infused distillate can be collected at any given strength and can be flavored and colored with permitted additives, both natural and artificial.

London Gin

This type of gin is made using a high-grade neutral spirit of at least 96 percent ABV, which is redistilled in a traditional still in the presence of the natural flavorings. The resulting distillate must have a minimum strength of 70 percent ABV. No artificial sweeteners, colorings, or flavors can be added.

Within the three categories of Gin, Distilled Gin, and London Gin are found the various styles of gin that we see on the shelves.

London Dry and Dry Gins

This type of gin falls into the London Gin category. It made its debut after the invention of the Coffey/column still in the 1830s. This was the birth of the clean, neutral spirit that enabled the creation of a purer gin. With a cleaner base spirit, distillers discovered that they no longer needed to mask the flavors in their distillates with sweeteners and other additives—and so Dry Gin was born. It was originally made solely in London, but is now made across the world, with many Dry Gins produced in the United States. Dry Gin is arguably the cleanest and purest style of gin available.

Old Tom Gin

Falling into the Distilled Gin category, Old Tom was the forerunner of London Dry. Prior to the column still, distillers in London were using various types of pot stills, some with little skill. Without the correct technical expertise, the distillate from these pot stills would have often tasted somewhat grim. To combat the unpleasant flavor, other ingredients were added after distillation to mask the taste. Today, Old Tom gins, like all gin, is seeing a revival. It is typically sweeter than dry styles due to the small amounts of added sugar.

Compound Gins

This type of gin falls into the Gin category. Compound Gins are made by mixing the juniper and botanicals with the neutral base spirit. It traces its origins back to the times of Prohibition and illicit liquor production. Despite being generally deemed inferior, advances in compounding have created significantly better Compound Gins. Some gins of this style are now performing well within the beverages trade and liquor competitions.

Geographically Indicated Gins

This type of gin can fall into any of the three categories mentioned above. Some wines can only be made in specific areas, and this can also be true for gin. Xoriguer from Menorca, Spain, and Vilnius Dzinas from Lithuania have protected geographical status. Plymouth Gin was one of these, but its status expired in 2015.

Barrel-Aged Gins

This gin can fall into any of the three gin categories. Now becoming increasingly popular, Barrel-Aged Gins undergo a period of time maturing in oak casks. The casks have, in most cases, been previously used to store whiskey.

Sloe Gin

Fruit has always been a natural partner to gin, and Sloe Gins can be traced back to the earliest English gins. Due to the large amounts of sloes and sugar, sloe gins are technically liqueurs. They are made by steeping large quantities of ripe sloe berries in the gin. They can be bottled at a lower minimum strength of 25 percent ABV.

How to
NOSE and TASTE GIN

Understanding gin

Gin is rarely drunk neat. In a quality gin bar, it will almost certainly be served over ice, garnished, and presented alongside a bottle of chilled bubbling tonic. Just perfect.

However, if you really want to discover the characteristics of a gin, it is worth taking a few moments to nose and taste the alcohol neat, and, in the same way as the tasting of all high-quality and flavorsome liquors, this nosing and tasting process can take practice.

Tasting strong liquor neat can be something of a shock to the senses, especially if you are new to the idea, but by following a few key tips, your senses will soon start to get in gear and reveal the sublime flavors that are hiding behind a mask of alcohol.

Nosing

Nosing is a good way to adapt your senses to the strength of the liquor. It is best done with a nosing glass, but you can use a snifter or wine glass. Take a modest measure of gin at room temperature, hold the glass a short distance away from your nose, and begin to nose it, breathing in the aromas. After a few seconds, take the glass away and take a few moments to breathe in and out normally. Then bring the glass back, nose it again, and repeat the process.

Do this a few times, taking breaks, and your olfactory senses will start to get used to the strength and, slowly, you will start to unravel the aromas in your gin. After a few minutes it will seem like a different drink. It's all to do with adapting your senses.

Tasting

You need to take time when tasting liquors neat. Those unfamiliar with strong alcohol will instinctively want to swallow the liquor after just a fraction of a second on the palate, in the same way that they might drink beer or wine. When liquors are tasted in this way, however, it can lead to an unpleasant bite and a coarse, burning feeling on the throat and senses.

You can avoid this by tasting the liquor in a different way. Visualize a small teaspoon of liquid, roll it onto your tongue, and hold it there. Then roll it around your mouth, coating your tongue, again holding the alcohol for a few seconds. This may feel strange at first, but you will get used to strength and start to find flavor. After the first sip, take a few moments and then revisit the glass. Upon tasting the second and third time, the alcohol and prickliness will have subsided and you will start to discover much more character and flavor.

While nosing and tasting, try to think about how the flavors reveal themselves and the liquor's texture. This more analytical approach to tasting gin can be rewarding, especially when you are comparing different gins. But where gin really performs is when it is lengthened in the classic "G&T" (gin and tonic) or in a cocktail

Tonic

When adding tonic water to gin, start small and build up. A two-to-one ratio is a good place to start. Like adding salt to food, you can always add more but you can't take it away. A good-quality tonic water is of critical importance—adding flat, lifeless, cheap tonic water to good gin is an abomination to serious mixologists and should be avoided at all costs. A handful of key brands have started to lead the way over the last few years and have become widely available in supermarkets.

Today, many flavored tonic waters can also be found, some of which work well with specific gins. Alongside new flavored tonic waters, signature serves and elaborate garnishes have become common practice in many bars, because gin brands are eager to find a unique selling point for their product. Through this, an almost infinite number of serves have emerged, some that work well, and others that don't. Remember it is the gin that should be bringing the character and flavor to your G&T, not a handful of fruit, leaves, or seeds.

By far the most important part of tasting any gin, whether neat, with tonic, or in a cocktail, is enjoyment. Drink your gin how YOU like it, and don't let anyone tell you otherwise.

GLASSWARE

Presentation is everything in mixology, so it is important to serve a cocktail in the appropriate glass—the size, shape, and style all have an impact on the visual perception and enjoyment of the drink. Here are some of the classic glasses that you will need to have in your collection.

Martini glass

The most iconic of all cocktail glasses, the conical martini glass emerged with the art deco movement. The long stem is perfect for chilled drinks, because it keeps people's hands from inadvertently warming the cocktail.

Highball glass

Sometimes also known as a Collins glass, these glasses are perfect for serving drinks with a high proportion of mixer to alcohol. The highball glass is versatile enough to be a substitute for the similarly shaped, but slightly larger, Collins glass.

Old-fashioned glass

The lowball glass, also known as a rocks glass, is a short, squat tumbler and is great for serving any alcohol on the rocks, or for short, mixed cocktails.

Champagne flute

The tall, thin flute's tapered design reduces the champagne's surface area and so helps to keep the fizz in the drink for longer. The flute has now largely replaced the coupe glass for serving champagne and champagne cocktails.

Shot glass

This glass is a home-bar essential and can hold just enough alcohol to be drunk in one mouthful. It also has a firm base that can be satisfyingly slammed on a bar top. The shot glass can also stand in for a measure when making cocktails.

Margarita glass

The Margarita, or coupette, glass, as its name implies, was designed specifically for serving Margaritas. It is ideal for any frozen, blended drinks.

Coupe glass

A wide-rim glass that is good for serving sparkling drinks, it was once the glass of choice for champagne. Legend has it that the glass is modeled on a woman's breast.

Snifter glass

The bowl-shape snifter glass invites drinkers to cradle the drink in their hands, warming the contents of the glass, so it is good for winter liquors, such as brandy. The aroma of the drink is held in the glass, allowing you to breathe in the drink before sipping.

Hurricane glass

This pear-shaped glass pays homage to the hurricane lamp and was the glass used to create the New Orleans rum-based cocktail, the Hurricane. It's also used for a variety of frozen and blended cocktails.

Iced beverage glass

A variation on the highball glass that combines a tapered, tall bowl with a short stem, this glass is ideal for serving chilled drinks such as the Singapore Sling and Long Island Ice Tea.

MIXOLOGY
EQUIPMENT

The equipment you have in your home bar depends on whether you are a cocktail king or queen who likes all the latest gadgets, or whether you are prepared to make do with some basic options. Nowadays, there is no limit to the amount of bar equipment available, but you definitely won't need a lot of gimicky gadgets to make the majority of the drinks in this book. Here is an outline of the essential tools of the trade.

Jiggers

A jigger (see opposite, top) is a bartender's basic measuring tool and is essential for crafting the perfect blend of ingredients. It usually has a measurement on each end, such as 1 ounce and 1½ ounces. Look for a steel jigger with clear measurement markings so you can easily and accurately pour out the measures.

Bar spoon

A proper bar spoon has a small bowl and a long handle that allows you to muddle, mix, and stir with ease. Spoons come in a variety of lengths and widths, and a stylish bar spoon is an attractive addition to any bartender's equipment.

Shaker

Most contemporary shakers are made from steel, because steel doesn't tarnish readily and doesn't conduct heat easily—this is useful for chilled cocktails, because the ice cools the cocktail instead of the shaker. Most standard shakers come with a built-in strainer, but if you're using a Boston or Parisian shaker, you'll need to use a separate strainer.

Mixing glass

Any vessel that holds about 2 cups of liquid can be used for mixing drinks. It is good to have a mixing glass with a spout or ridged rim so that you can stop ice from slipping into the glass; however, this is not vital, because you can always use a strainer. Mixing glasses are increasingly popular, and they are usually made of glass or crystal.

Muddler

For mashing up citrus fruit or crushing herbs, you need a muddler. This is a chunky wooden tool with a rounded end, and it can also be used to make cracked ice. You can mash fruit or crush herbs with a mortar and pestle, but the advantage of a muddler is that it can be used directly in the mixing glass.

Strainer

A bar or Hawthorne strainer (see right, far right) is an essential tool to prevent ice and other ingredients from being poured into your glass. Some cocktails need to be double strained, so even if there is a strainer in your cocktail shaker, you'll still need a separate Hawthorne strainer in your bar collection.

Juicer

A traditional juicer, with a ridged half-lemon shape on a saucer, works well for juicing small amounts. There is also a citrus spout available that screws into a lemon or lime; it is useful for obtaining tiny amounts of juice. Mechanical or electric presses are great for large amounts of juice, but they are not essential in a home bar.

Other equipment

Other items you might need in your home-bar equipment are a corkscrew, bottle opener, decorative toothpicks, blender, tongs, ice bucket, cutting board, knives, pitchers, swizzle sticks, straws, and an espuma gun for making foams.

MIXING TECHNIQUES

Shaking and stirring

These are the two most basic mixology techniques, and they are essential to master in order to confidently make a range of both classic and craft cocktails.

Shaking is when you add all the ingredients, with the specified amount of ice cubes, to the shaker and shake vigorously for 5–10 seconds. The benefits of shaking are that the drink is rapidly mixed, chilled, and aerated. Once the drink has been shaken, the outside of the shaker should be lightly frosted.

Shaking a cocktail will dilute your drink significantly. This is an essential part of the cocktail-making process and gives recipes the correct balance of taste, strength, and temperature. After shaking, the drink is double strained into glasses—the shaker should have an inbuilt strainer, but you will usually also use a separate strainer over the glass. Shaking can also be used to prepare cocktails that include an ingredient that will not combine with less vigorous forms of mixing, such as an egg white.

Stirring is the purist's choice. This is a mixing technique where you add all the ingredients, usually with some ice cubes, but you combine them in a mixing glass and then stir the ingredients together using a long-handled bar spoon or swizzle stick. As with shaking, this allows for you to blend and chill the ingredients without too much erosion of the ice, so you can control the level of dilution and keep it to a minimum. This simple technique is vital for drinks that do not need a lot of dilution, such as the classic Dry Martini.

Building and layering

Building is a mixology technique, explaining the task of pouring all the ingredients, one by one, usually over ice, into the serving glass. You might then stir the cocktail briefly, but this is just to mix instead of to chill or aerate. You need to follow built recipes exactly, because the order of the ingredients can change from drink to drink and this can affect the final flavor.

Another important bartending skill is the art of layering, requiring concentration, precision, and a steady hand. To make layered shooters or other drinks, you generally pour the heaviest liquid first, working through to the lightest. However, the real trick is the technique. Either touch the top of the drink with a long-handle bar spoon and pour the liquid slowly over the back of it to disperse it across the top of the ingredients already in the glass, or pour the liquid down the twisted stem that many bar spoons have. You should hold the spoon's flat disk just above the drink. Be sure to use a clean bar spoon for each layer. Floating is the term used to describe adding the top layer.

Muddling and blending

Muddling is the extraction of the juice or oils from the pulp or skin of a fruit, herb, or spice. It involves mashing ingredients to release their flavors and it's usually done with a wooden pestle-like implement called a muddler. The end that is used to crush ingredients is thicker and rounded, and the opposite, thinner end is used to stir. The best muddling technique is to keep pressing down with a twisting action until the ingredient has released all its oil or juice. If you don't have a muddler, use a mortar and pestle or the end of a wooden spoon.

As the name suggests, blending is when all the cocktail ingredients are combined in a blender or food processor. This technique is often used when mixing alcohol with fruit or with creamy ingredients that do not combine well unless they are blended. These drinks are often blended with crushed or cracked ice to produce cocktails with a smooth, frozen consistency.

Foams and airs

Foams and airs can be created in various thicknesses, from a light froth to a heavy, creamy foam. For a simple foam, use egg white, lemon juice, and sugar. To top two cocktails, whisk 1 egg white with ½ ounce of lemon juice and 1 teaspoon of superfine sugar until thoroughly mixed. Put the mixture into an espuma gun or cream whipper, then charge, shake, and spray it over the top of the cocktails for a light, creamy finish. The fresher the egg white, the more stable the foam, so use fresh eggs.

An air is an extremely light froth with an effervescent texture that is less heavy than a foam—it can range from a bubble bath foam to the fizz on the top of a glass of champagne. To make a light air, the best ingredient to use is lecithin. Simply whisk a pinch of powdered lecithin with sugar syrup using a handheld immersion blender or electric mixer until a light air is created. If you prefer a finer air, use a milk frother.

can always use a strainer. Mixing glasses are increasingly popular, and they are usually made of glass or crystal.

Muddler

For mashing up citrus fruit or crushing herbs, you need a muddler. This is a chunky wooden tool with a rounded end, and it can also be used to make cracked ice. You can mash fruit or crush herbs with a mortar and pestle, but the advantage of a muddler is that it can be used directly in the mixing glass.

Strainer

A bar or Hawthorne strainer (see right, far right) is an essential tool to prevent ice and other ingredients from being poured into your glass. Some cocktails need to be double strained, so even if there is a strainer in your cocktail shaker, you'll still need a separate Hawthorne strainer in your bar collection.

Juicer

A traditional juicer, with a ridged half-lemon shape on a saucer, works well for juicing small amounts. There is also a citrus spout available that screws into a lemon or lime; it is useful for obtaining tiny amounts of juice. Mechanical or electric presses are great for large amounts of juice, but they are not essential in a home bar.

Other equipment

Other items you might need in your home-bar equipment are a corkscrew, bottle opener, decorative toothpicks, blender, tongs, ice bucket, cutting board, knives, pitchers, swizzle sticks, straws, and an espuma gun for making foams.

MIXING TECHNIQUES

Shaking and stirring

These are the two most basic mixology techniques, and they are essential to master in order to confidently make a range of both classic and craft cocktails.

Shaking is when you add all the ingredients, with the specified amount of ice cubes, to the shaker and shake vigorously for 5–10 seconds. The benefits of shaking are that the drink is rapidly mixed, chilled, and aerated. Once the drink has been shaken, the outside of the shaker should be lightly frosted.

Shaking a cocktail will dilute your drink significantly. This is an essential part of the cocktail-making process and gives recipes the correct balance of taste, strength, and temperature. After shaking, the drink is double strained into glasses—the shaker should have an inbuilt strainer, but you will usually also use a separate strainer over the glass. Shaking can also be used to prepare cocktails that include an ingredient that will not combine with less vigorous forms of mixing, such as an egg white.

Stirring is the purist's choice. This is a mixing technique where you add all the ingredients, usually with some ice cubes, but you combine them in a mixing glass and then stir the ingredients together using a long-handled bar spoon or swizzle stick. As with shaking, this allows for you to blend and chill the ingredients without too much erosion of the ice, so you can control the level of dilution and keep it to a minimum. This simple technique is vital for drinks that do not need a lot of dilution, such as the classic Dry Martini.

Chapter 1

◆

SIMPLE KEYS

The making of a cocktail is part of the whole gin mixology experience, but there are occasions when you want to produce a refreshing cocktail in an eminently smooth, no-fuss manner. Fewer ingredients help with this aspiration. Here are some ideas with a maximum of three key components, from a London French 75 to a Topaz Martini.

FROZEN G&T

Serves 1

Ingredients

1¾ ounces gin

5 ounces tonic water

lime wedge, to garnish

1. Fill a Collins or highball glass with crushed ice.

2. Pour in the gin. Top with tonic water. Garnish with the lime wedge and serve immediately.

VESPERS

Serves 1

Ingredients

1 ¼ ounces gin, iced

¾ ounce vodka, iced

½ ounce dry vermouth
or Lillet

lemon peel, to garnish

1. Shake the liquid ingredients over ice until frosted. Strain into a frosted martini glass. Garnish with lemon peel and serve immediately.

LONDON FRENCH 75

Ingredients

1¾ ounces London gin

¾ ounce lemon juice

chilled champagne

1. Shake the gin and lemon juice vigorously over cracked ice until well frosted.

2. Strain into a chilled glass and top up with champagne. Serve immediately.

NAVY STRENGTH

◆

Long voyages, stormy swells, inclement weather, and the perpetual threat of enemy cannons—it is enough to make anyone reach for a strong drink. But it wasn't the extreme circumstances and sailors' thirst that led to such strong gin and other alcohol being taken aboard naval ships.

Most naval vessels stored their alcohol below deck in a secure part of the ship, under the watchful eye of a commanding officer. These secure caches also held the ship's gunpowder. This meant that higher-strength gin was required for the navy so the gin-soaked powder would still ignite in the event of a spillage. It also ensured that the alcohol had a certain level of quality and had not been watered down.

The use of gunpowder is one of the earliest methods of measuring the alcoholic strength of liquor. A few grains of gunpowder would be mixed with the alcohol and ignited. If the liquor was above 57.15 percent ABV, the gunpowder would ignite and the liquor would be proven— this led to the term "proof" being used as a measure of strength. It was not just the British navy that used the gunpowder method, but tax collectors and merchants, too. Any liquor synonymous with the navy usually has navy-strength variations available.

GIBSON

Serves 1
Ingredients

2½ ounces gin

¾ ounce dry vermouth

cocktail onions, to garnish

1. Fill a cocktail glass with cracked ice and pour the gin and vermouth over it. Garnish with two or three cocktail onions and serve immediately.

SLOE SCREW

Serves 1
Ingredients

1¾ ounces sloe gin
orange juice
orange slice, to garnish

1. Shake the sloe gin and orange juice over cracked ice until well frosted and pour into a chilled glass.

2. Garnish with the orange slice and serve immediately.

SILVER STREAK

Serves 1
Ingredients

¾ ounce gin, iced

¾ ounce kümmel, iced

1. Fill a small old-fashioned glass or tumbler with ice cubes and pour in the gin. Slowly pour on the kümmel and serve immediately.

ALASKA

Serves 1
Ingredients

½ ounce gin
½ ounce yellow Chartreuse

1. Shake the gin and Chartreuse over ice cubes until well frosted.

2. Strain into a chilled glass and serve immediately.

TOPAZ MARTINI

Serves 1

Ingredients

1¾ ounces gin

½ ounce orange curaçao

orange-peel twist,
to garnish

1. Put some cracked ice into a mixing glass. Pour the gin and orange curaçao over the ice. Stir well to mix, then strain into a chilled cocktail glass.

2. Garnish with a twist of orange peel and serve immediately.

GREEN LADY

Serves 1
Ingredients

1¾ ounces gin
¾ ounce green Chartreuse
dash lime juice

1. Shake the liquid ingredients vigorously over ice until well frosted.

2. Strain into a chilled cocktail glass and serve immediately.

RACKET
CLUB

Serves 1
Ingredients

dash orange bitters

¾ ounce gin

¾ ounce vermouth

orange-peel twist, to garnish

1. Dash the orange bitters over ice in a mixing glass and pour in the gin and vermouth. Stir well to mix, then strain into a chilled cocktail glass. Garnish with a twist of orange peel and serve immediately.

GLASS SLIPPER

Serves 1
Ingredients

2½ ounces gin

¾ ounce blue curaçao

1. Shake the gin and curaçao over ice until well frosted. Strain into a chilled cocktail glass. Serve immediately.

FIFTY FIFTY

Serves 1
Ingredients

1¾ ounces gin
1¾ ounces dry vermouth
cocktail olive, to garnish

1. Shake the gin and vermouth vigorously over ice until well frosted. Strain into a chilled cocktail glass, garnish with an olive, and serve immediately.

SEVENTH HEAVEN

Serves 1
Ingredients

1¾ ounces gin

½ ounce maraschino
liqueur

½ ounce grapefruit juice

fresh mint sprigs,
to garnish

1. Shake all the liquid ingredients vigorously over ice cubes until well frosted.

2. Strain into a chilled cocktail glass. Garnish with fresh mint and serve immediately.

PALM BEACH

Serves 1
Ingredients

¾ ounce gin

¾ ounce white rum

¾ ounce pineapple juice

1. Shake the gin, rum, and pineapple juice vigorously over cracked ice until well frosted.

2. Strain into a chilled glass and serve immediately.

ORANGE GIN SLING

Serves 1
Ingredients

1¾ ounces gin
4 dashes orange bitters

1. Pour the gin into a cocktail glass, then carefully splash on the orange bitters. Serve immediately.

SAKETINI

Serves 1
Ingredients

2½ ounces gin

½ ounce sake

lemon-peel twist, to garnish

1. Shake the gin and sake vigorously over ice until well frosted.

2. Strain into a chilled cocktail glass and garnish with a twist of lemon peel. Serve immediately.

Chapter 2

---◆---

CLASSIC CHORDS

Classic gin cocktails demand a sense of occasion. Think of 007's defining Vesper Martini; Gin Rickey, the refreshing, cooling drink in *The Great Gatsby*; the Gimlet, which made its debut in Raymond Chandler's 1950s novel *The Long Goodbye*; and the quintessentially English Pink Gin, a favorite in the novels of Agatha Christie and John Le Carré.

MARTINI

Serves 1

Ingredients

2½ ounces gin

1 teaspoon dry vermouth,
or to taste

cocktail olive, to garnish

1. Put four to six ice cubes, cracked, into a
cocktail shaker.

2. Pour the gin and vermouth over the ice.

3. Shake until well frosted. Strain into
a chilled cocktail glass.

4. Garnish with the olive. Serve immediately.

NEGRONI

Serves 1

Ingredients

¾ ounce gin

¾ ounce Campari

½ ounce sweet vermouth

orange-peel twist,
to garnish

1. Put some cracked ice into a mixing glass. Pour the gin, Campari, and vermouth over the ice and stir well to mix.

2. Strain into a chilled glass and garnish with an orange-peel twist. Serve immediately.

PINK
GIN

Serves 1
Ingredients

¾ ounce Plymouth Gin

few drops Angostura
bitters

¾ ounce water, iced

maraschino cherry,
to decorate

1. Pour the first three ingredients into
a mixing glass and stir.

2. Strain into a cocktail glass and garnish with
a maraschino cherry. Serve immediately.

GIN RICKEY

Serves 1

Ingredients

1¾ ounces gin

¾ ounce lime juice

club soda

lemon slice, to garnish

1. Fill a chilled highball glass or goblet with cracked ice.

2. Pour the gin and lime juice over the ice.

3. Top with club soda.

4. Stir gently to mix and garnish with a lemon slice. Serve immediately.

DUTCH COURAGE

Those experiencing preshow nerves before a performance or presentation usually welcome a strong drink. The phrase "Dutch courage" comes from the Low Countries (modern-day Netherlands, Belgium, parts of northern France, and Germany), the birthplace of genever (the grandfather of modern gin) and the Thirty Years' War of 1618–1638.

The Thirty Years' War was Europe's last major religious war centered around the Protestant Reformation, and was a bloody, brutal, and drawn-out affair involving several great powers in Europe. It also had lasting effects. In the early stages of the war, English soldiers were sent by Queen Elizabeth I to support Protestant forces fighting against the Catholic-led armies of the Holy Roman Empire. They stood side by side with the Dutch military and received genever to fortify themselves during battle. Troops who returned home are believed to have told tales of the "Dutch Courage" that drove them to overcome their fears and foes on the battlefield, sowing the seeds of a love affair with juniper and gin that continues to this day.

CLOVER CLUB

Serves 1
Ingredients

1¾ ounces gin

¾ ounce lime juice

¾ ounce grenadine

1 egg white

1. Pour all ingredients over ice. Shake vigorously until well frosted. Strain into a chilled cocktail glass and serve immediately.

GIN SLING

Serves 1
Ingredients

1 sugar cube

¾ ounce gin

freshly grated nutmeg

lemon slice, to serve

1. Place the sugar in an old-fashioned glass and add 4 ounces of hot water. Stir until the sugar is dissolved.

2. Stir in the gin, sprinkle with nutmeg, and serve immediately with a slice of lemon.

SINGAPORE
SLING

Serves 1
Ingredients

1¾ ounces gin

¾ ounce cherry brandy

¾ ounce lemon juice

1 teaspoon grenadine

club soda

lime peel strips and
cocktail cherries,
to garnish

1. Put four to six ice cubes, cracked, into
a cocktail shaker and pour the gin over the ice.

2. Pour in the cherry brandy, lemon juice,
and grenadine and shake vigorously until
well frosted.

3. Fill a chilled glass halfway with cracked ice
and strain the cocktail over the ice.

4. Top with club soda and garnish with the
lime peel and cherries. Serve immediately.

SMOKED LAST WORD

Serves 1

Ingredients

¾ ounce smoked gin

¾ ounce lime juice

¾ ounce maraschino liqueur

¾ ounce green Chartreuse

lime slice, to garnish

SMOKED GIN

3½ ounces whiskey barrel wood chips

1½ cups gin

1. To make the smoked gin, lay the wood chips on a metal tray and put the tray onto a heatproof, preferably metal, surface. Using a chef's blowtorch, scorch the wood chips until about 50 percent of them have blackened.

2. Place the scorched wood chips in a sterilized and sealable, medium-size jar. Pour in the gin, and keep the gin bottle. Seal the jar and let steep in a cool place for two weeks.

3. Strain the gin through a coffee filter and pour back into its bottle.

4. For the cocktail, put all the ingredients except the lime slice into a cocktail shaker. Shake well and double strain into a coupe glass. Garnish with the lime slice and serve.

ORANGE BLOSSOM

Serves 1
Ingredients

1¾ ounces gin

¾ ounces orange juice

orange slices, to garnish

1. Shake the gin and orange juice vigorously over cracked ice until well frosted. Strain into a chilled cocktail glass and garnish with orange slices. Serve immediately.

GIMLET

Serves 1
Ingredients

¾ ounce gin

½ ounce fresh lime juice

tonic water

lime slices, to decorate

1. Pour the gin and lime juice over ice in a chilled old-fashioned glass. Top with tonic water and garnish with slices of lime. Serve immediately.

MARTINEZ

Serves 1
Ingredients

¾ ounces gin, iced

¾ ounce Italian vermouth

dash Angostura bitters

dash maraschino liqueur

twisted lemon slice,
to garnish

1. Shake the gin, vermouth, bitters, and maraschino over ice until frosted. Strain into a chilled cocktail glass and garnish with a twisted lemon slice. Serve immediately.

LONG ISLAND ICED TEA

Serves 1

Ingredients

¾ ounce vodka

¾ ounce gin

¾ ounce white tequila

¾ ounce white rum

½ ounce white crème
de menthe

¾ ounces lemon juice

1 teaspoon superfine sugar

cola

lime wedge, to garnish

1. Put four to six ice cubes, cracked, into a cocktail shaker. Pour all the liquid ingredients except the cola over the ice, add the sugar, and shake vigorously until well frosted.

2. Fill a tall glass halfway with cracked ice and strain over the cocktail. Top with cola, garnish with the lime wedge, and serve immediately.

BRONX

Serves 1
Ingredients

¾ ounces gin

¾ ounce orange juice

½ ounce dry vermouth

½ ounce sweet vermouth

1. Pour the gin, orange juice, dry vermouth, and sweet vermouth over cracked ice in a mixing glass. Stir to mix and strain into a chilled cocktail glass. Serve immediately.

ALABAMA SLAMMER

Serves 1
Ingredients

¾ ounce Southern Comfort

¾ ounce Amaretto

¾ ounce sloe gin

½ teaspoon lemon juice

1. Pour the Southern Comfort, Amaretto, and sloe gin over cracked ice in a mixing glass and stir.

2. Strain into a shot glass and add the lemon juice. Cover with your hand, slam on the table, and drink immediately.

TOM COLLINS

Serves 1
Ingredients

2½ ounces gin

¾ ounces lemon juice

½ ounce sugar syrup

club soda

lemon slices, to garnish

1. Put four to six ice cubes, cracked, into a cocktail shaker.

2. Pour the gin, lemon juice, and sugar syrup over the ice and shake vigorously until well frosted.

3. Strain into a chilled Collins glass.

4. Top with club soda and garnish with the lemon slices. Serve immediately.

MAIDEN'S PRAYER

Serves 1
Ingredients

¾ ounce gin

¾ ounce triple sec

1 teaspoon orange juice

1 teaspoon lemon juice

lemon peel twist, to decorate

1. Shake all the ingredients vigorously over ice until well frosted.

2. Strain into a chilled cocktail glass and decorate with the twist of lemon peel. Serve immediately.

Chapter 3

CITRUS NOTES

Citrus has a strong association with cocktails—the fresh acidity of orange, lemon, lime, and grapefruit typically balances out the sweeter and richer components within a cocktail. This is clearly demonstrated by the fact that gin cocktails with a zing of citrus simply cannot be restricted to the parameters of this chapter.

GIN, CHAMPAGNE & GRAPEFRUIT SORBET

Serves 6

Ingredients

1 cup superfine sugar

3½ ounces water

7 ounces ruby grapefruit juice

6 scoops grapefruit sorbet

5 ounces gin

12 splashes rhubarb bitters

1 (750-milliliter) bottle champagne

6 grapefruit-peel twists, to garnish

1. You will need an ice-cream maker for this recipe. Gently heat the sugar and water in a medium saucepan until the sugar has dissolved. Remove from the heat and let cool slightly, then add the grapefruit juice.

2. Place the grapefruit mixture in an ice-cream maker and churn until frozen. Once frozen, transfer the sorbet to a plastic container and place in the freezer for a couple of hours until completely firm.

3. When ready to serve, divide the sorbet among six cocktail glasses, followed by the gin and rhubarb bitters. Top each glass with the champagne and garnish with the grapefruit peel. Serve immediately.

MATCHA GREEN TEA COCKTAIL

Serves 1

Ingredients

1 egg white

½ ounce lime juice

1 teaspoon superfine sugar

¾ ounce green tea and lemon grass gin

¾ ounce sake

½ ounce agave syrup

½ ounce lime juice

ice cubes

GREEN TEA AND LEMONGRASS GIN

1½ cups gin

1 teaspoon matcha green tea powder

2 fresh lemongrass stalks, coarsely chopped

1. The green tea and lemongrass gin takes 24 hours to steep. To make the foam, you will need an espuma gun.

2. To make the gin, pour the gin into a sterilized and sealable, medium-sized jar. Keep the gin bottle for later use. Add the matcha green tea and lemongrass. Mix well, then seal and let steep for 24 hours.

3. After 24 hours, strain the mixture through a coffee filter and pour back into the reserved gin bottle. It will keep for several months.

4. For the cocktail, lightly whisk the egg white, lime juice, and sugar in a medium bowl until the sugar has dissolved. Pour the egg mixture into an espuma gun and charge once.

5. Put the green tea gin, sake, agave syrup, and lime juice into a cocktail shaker filled with ice cubes. Shake vigorously until well frosted, then double-strain into an ice-filled coupe glass. Shake the espuma gun and top the cocktail with the egg foam. Serve immediately.

GRAPEFRUIT & CHERRY G&T

Serves 1

Ingredients

1 slice of grapefruit

4 cherries, pitted

1¾ ounces gin

6 ounces tonic water

2 cherries, to garnish

1. Cut the grapefruit slice into chunks. Put the grapefruit and cherries into a cocktail shaker.

2. Using a muddler, crush the grapefruit and cherries for about 30 seconds to release the flavors and oils.

3. Add the gin to the cocktail shaker and stir. Pour the mixture into a Collins or highball glass.

4. Add some ice cubes to the glass and top with tonic water.

5. Decorate with cherries on top and serve immediately.

STREGA
SOUR

Serves 1

Ingredients

1 ¾ ounces gin

¾ ounce Strega

¾ ounce lemon juice

lemon slice, to decorate

1. Shake the gin, Strega, and lemon juice vigorously over ice until well frosted. Strain into a cocktail glass and garnish with a slice of lemon. Serve immediately.

LEAPFROG

Serves 1

Ingredients

juice of ½ lemon

1¾ ounces gin

ginger ale

orange slice, to garnish

1. Chill a long tumbler and then add 1 ice cube, the lemon juice, and gin. Stir just once.

2. Top with ginger ale to taste and garnish with a slice of orange. Serve immediately.

MOTHER'S RUIN

The Gin Craze that swept through London in the early eighteenth century saw debauchery and depravity on an unprecedented scale. Life was hard, living conditions were appalling, and the poor had little to aspire to. Coupled with a tidal wave of cheap gin, the stage was set for a "bender" on a monumental scale.

During this period, gin production grew dramatically. By the 1730s, there was enough gin being made to support a 600,000-strong London population, supplying around 14 gallons per person per year. Gin was made using questionable methods, laced with other ingredients to mask the foul flavors emanating from the distillate. It was cheaper than beer, incredibly strong, and available in every shop and filth-ridden alleyway.

By 1723, the death rate in London outweighed the birthrate. Gin became heavily identified with women and adopted one of its best-known synonyms, Mother's Ruin. The government stepped in, but its efforts failed and in some cases made the situation worse. It took until the 1760s for the city to start to sober up.

MOONLIGHT

Serves 4
Ingredients

2½ ounces grapefruit juice

3½ ounces gin

¾ ounce kirsch

3½ ounces white wine

½ teaspoon lemon zest

1. Shake all the liquid ingredients vigorously over ice cubes until well frosted. Strain into chilled glasses and serve immediately.

GRAND ROYAL CLOVER CLUB

Serves 1
Ingredients

1¾ ounces gin

¾ ounce lemon juice

¾ ounce grenadine

1 egg white

lime-peel twist, to garnish

1. Pour the first four ingredients over ice.

2. Shake vigorously until well frosted and strain into a chilled cocktail glass.

3. Garnish with a twist of lime peel and serve immediately.

BEE'S KNEES

Serves 1
Ingredients

¾ ounce gin
¼ ounce fresh lemon juice
½ ounce honey
bitter lemon, to taste
lemon zest, to garnish

1. Shake the first three ingredients over ice until well frosted. Strain into a tall, ice-filled glass and top with bitter lemon.

2. Garnish with a few shreds of lemon zest. Serve immediately.

FIREFLY

Serves 1
Ingredients

¾ ounce gin

½ ounce tequila

½ ounce dry orange curaçao

½ ounce lemon juice

dash egg white

orange peel, to garnish

1. Shake all the liquid ingredients well over ice until frosted.

2. Strain into a chilled cocktail glass and garnish with a twist of orange peel. Serve immediately.

STRESSED
OUT

Serves 1

Ingredients

¾ ounce gin, iced

½ ounce green Chartreuse, iced

½ ounce lime juice, chilled

dash pastis, iced

sugar syrup, to taste

lime wedge, to garnish

1. Stir all the liquid ingredients together over ice cubes until well frosted.

2. Strain into a small cocktail glass filled with crushed ice and add a lime wedge. Serve immediately.

BULLDOG

Serves 1
Ingredients

1¾ ounces gin

¾ ounce fresh orange juice

ginger ale

orange slice

1. Stir the gin and orange juice over ice in a medium tumbler. Top with ginger ale and add a slice of orange. Serve immediately.

BRIDE'S MOTHER

Serves 1
Ingredients

1¼ ounces sloe gin

¾ ounce gin

2 ounces grapefruit juice

½ ounce sugar syrup

grapefruit slices, to garnish

1. Shake the liquid ingredients vigorously over ice cubes until well frosted.

2. Strain over crushed ice and garnish with grapefruit slices. Serve immediately.

FALLEN ANGEL

Serves 1
Ingredients

1 dash Angostura bitters

juice of 1 lemon or lime

1¾ ounces gin

green crème de menthe

1. Shake the first three ingredients over ice and strain into a cocktail glass. Top with two dashes of crème de menthe at the last minute. Serve immediately.

SLOE KISS

Serves 1
Ingredients

½ ounce sloe gin

½ ounce Southern Comfort

¾ ounce vodka

1 teaspoon Amaretto

splash Galliano

orange juice

orange peel twist, to garnish

1. Put four to six ice cubes, cracked, into a cocktail shaker, pour the sloe gin, Southern Comfort, vodka, and Amaretto over them, and shake until well frosted.

2. Strain into a long, chilled glass filled with cracked ice. Splash on the Galliano.

3. Top with orange juice and garnish with the orange peel. Serve immediately.

HAWAIIAN ORANGE BLOSSOM

Serves 1
Ingredients

1¾ ounces gin

¾ ounce triple sec

1¾ ounces orange juice

¾ ounce pineapple juice

pineapple slices and leaves,
to decorate

1. Shake the liquid ingredients vigorously over ice until well frosted.

2. Strain into a chilled wine glass and serve immediately garnished with pineapple slices and leaves.

Chapter 4

— ◆ —

EXOTIC RHYTHMS

Glamorous, magical, bizarre, enticing—escape the everyday,
search for something different, and enter a wonder-
world of cocktail enchantment. Here, you'll find cherries,
pineapple, and pomegranate; coconut, cream, and yogurt; and
Frangelico, blackberry brandy, and maraschino. Break down
the barriers and be seduced by the otherworldly.

GREEK YOGURT
COCKTAIL

Serves 1

Ingredients

1¾ ounces gin

¾ ounce Frangelico

1 tablespoon Greek-style
yogurt

¾ ounce agave syrup

½ ripe nectarine, pitted

¾ ounce lemon juice

nectarine slice, to garnish

1. Put the gin, Frangelico, yogurt, agave syrup, nectarine, and lemon juice into a cocktail shaker.

2. Using a cocktail muddler, crush all the ingredients to a smooth pulp.

3. Fill a Collins or highball glass with crushed ice. Strain the cocktail over the ice.

4. Garnish with the nectarine slice and serve immediately.

GIN & COCONUT
COCKTAIL

Serves 4

Ingredients

2 tablespoons finely grated coconut flesh

3½ ounces gin

3½ ounces bourbon

1¾ ounces agave syrup

3½ ounces lime juice

2½ cups coconut water

4 lime slices, to garnish

1. In a dry, small skillet, gently toast the coconut until golden. Remove from the heat and let cool.

2. Grind the cooled coconut in a spice grinder until it becomes a fine powder. Set aside.

3. Put the gin, bourbon, agave syrup, lime juice, and coconut water into a pitcher and mix well.

4. Divide the gin mixture among four ice cube-filled Collins or highball glasses.

5. Garnish each cocktail with a teaspoon of coconut powder and the lime slices. Serve immediately.

GIN, CHERRY & APPLE SLUSHIE

Serves 4

Ingredients

1 cup pitted fresh cherries

¾ ounce lemon juice

¼ cup superfine sugar

6¾ ounces gin

2½ cups apple juice

1. Put the cherries, lemon juice, and sugar into a medium saucepan. Gently heat until the sugar has dissolved and the cherries have broken down. Remove from the heat and let cool for 5 minutes.

2. Once cooled, transfer the cherry mixture to a blender and blend until smooth. Push it through a fine-mesh stainer to make a puree.

3. Put the gin, cherry puree, apple juice, and four handfuls of ice cubes into the blender and blend until smooth.

4. Divide the slushie among four glasses and serve immediately.

HARLEM

Ingredients

1¾ ounces gin

1¼ ounces pineapple juice

1 teaspoon maraschino liqueur

1 tablespoon chopped fresh pineapple

lime leaf, to garnish

1. Shake the first four ingredients vigorously over ice until well frosted.

2. Strain into a small chilled tumbler and garnish with a lime leaf. Serve immediately.

MAGNOLIA BLOSSOM

Serves 1

Ingredients

1¾ ounces gin

¾ ounce lemon juice

¾ ounce light cream

1. Shake the ingredients vigorously over ice until well frosted.

2. Strain into a chilled cocktail glass and serve immediately.

SHAKEN, NOT STIRRED . . .

It's no secret that many of the world's greatest leaders, artists, musicians, and writers have been known to enjoy a gin or two. One of the most famous figures associated with gin is, of course, Ian Fleming's James Bond. Bond's taste for a martini has become legendary, and it has resulted in the classic line being the bane of many mixologists' careers.

The gin trail continues with J. K. Rowling's liking for G&T; F. Scott Fitzgerald, who had a soft spot for a Gin Rickey; Raymond Chandler, who favored a Gimlet; and Queen Elizabeth II, who is partial to a Gin and Dubonnet. So gin is woven into our history and culture.

Aside from the world of 007, the martini is actually better being stirred than being shaken. It avoids "bruising" the gin and overdiluting the drink, and it preserves the "mouthfeel" of the ingredients. The martini is, in fact, a wickedly strong cocktail, which traditionally contains a hefty amount of gin. It is the best drink to aid in an assassination—and one to assassinate your evening if you have too many! But, let's face it, if you held a "licence to kill" and were on the case of a maniacal villain, you would probably be after a stiff drink, too.

GOLDEN DAWN

Serves 1
Ingredients

½ ounce gin

½ ounce Calvados or other apple brandy

½ ounce apricot brandy

½ ounce mango juice

dash grenadine

1. Mix the first four ingredients together over ice.

2. Strain into a cocktail glass and gradually add the dash of grenadine so the color ripples through. Serve immediately.

TEARDROP

Serves 1

Ingredients

¾ ounce gin

1¾ ounces apricot nectar
or peach nectar

¾ ounce light cream

½ ounce strawberry syrup

fresh strawberry and peach
slices, to garnish

1. Put the gin, apricot nectar, and cream into a blender and blend for 5–10 seconds, until thick and frothy.

2. Pour into a long glass filled with crushed ice.

3. Splash the strawberry syrup on top and garnish with the strawberry and peach slices. Serve immediately.

TURKISH DELIGHT GIN COCKTAIL

Serves 1

Ingredients

1¾ ounces gin

6 ounces cranberry juice

1 tablespoon honey

¼ teaspoon rosewater

1 tablespoon pomegranate seeds

¼ teaspoon dried rose petals, plus extra to garnish

1. Pour the gin, cranberry juice, honey, and rosewater into a Collins or highball glass.

2. Stir with a bar spoon until the honey has dissolved.

3. Add a few ice cubes, the pomegranate seeds, and rose petals, then stir again.

4. Garnish with the rose petals and serve immediately with a straw.

POLISH SIDECAR

Serves 1
Ingredients

1¾ ounces gin

¾ ounce blackberry brandy

¾ ounce lemon juice

1. Pour the gin, blackberry brandy, and lemon juice over ice and shake vigorously until well frosted, then strain into a chilled cocktail glass. Serve immediately.

BLUE TRAIN

Serves 1
Ingredients

1¾ ounces gin

¾ ounce triple sec

¾ ounce lemon juice

splash blue curaçao

1. Pour all of the ingredients into a cocktail shaker filled with cracked ice.

2. Shake vigorously until frosted and strain into a chilled cocktail glass. Serve immediately.

WEDDING BELLE

Serves 1
Ingredients

1¾ ounces gin

1¾ ounces Dubonnet

¾ ounce cherry brandy

¾ ounce orange juice

orange-peel twist,
to garnish

1. Shake the liquid ingredients over ice cubes until well frosted.

serve immediately garnish with a twist of orange peel. Serve immediately.

BLUE BLOODED

Serves 1
Ingredients

¾ ounce gin

¾ ounce passion-fruit nectar

4 cubes melon or mango

1–2 teaspoons blue curaçao

1. Put the gin, passion-fruit nectar, melon cubes, and four to six ice cubes, cracked, into a blender and blend until smooth and frosted.

2. Pour into a tall, chilled glass filled with cracked ice and top with the curaçao. Serve immediately.

ALEXANDER

Serves 1

Ingredients

¾ ounce gin

¾ ounce crème de cacao

¾ ounce light cream

freshly grated nutmeg,
to garnish

1. Shake the first three ingredients vigorously over cracked ice until well frosted.

2. Strain into a chilled cocktail glass and garnish with grated nutmeg. Serve immediately.

FRUIT CRAZY

Serves 1
Ingredients

¾ ounce gin

½ ounce melon liqueur

¾ ounce mango nectar

¾ ounce grapefruit juice

1 medium egg white

mango slice, to garnish

1. Shake the first five ingredients together over ice cubes until frosted.

2. Strain into a chilled long glass with more ice to fill, and garnish with a slice of mango. Serve immediately.

PUSSYCAT

Serves 1
Ingredients

dash grenadine

1¾ ounces gin

pineapple juice

pineapple slice, to garnish

1. Fill a chilled tumbler halfway with cracked ice.

2. Dash the grenadine over the ice and add the gin.

3. Top with pineapple juice and garnish with the pineapple slice. Serve immediately.

1¾ ounces gin

¾ ounce sweet vermouth

¾ ounce dry vermouth

3 strawberries, plus
1 strawberry to garnish

2. Add four to six ice cubes, cracked. Blend until smooth.

3. Pour into a chilled cocktail glass and garnish with the remaining strawberry. Serve immediately.

Chapter 5

❖

HEADY BEATS

Ready for a pulsating experience? It's time to be transported by the splendor of a convivial cocktail. From Mango & Black Pepper Cocktail and Rolls-Royce 2 to Spiced Whiskey Sour and Old Etonian, and featuring everything from dark rum and Grand Marnier to crème de noyaux, prepare yourself for a heady ride.

MANGO & BLACK PEPPER COCKTAIL

Serves 1

Ingredients

¾ ounce gin

¾ ounce dark rum

1 teaspoon packed light
brown sugar

¾ ounce lime juice

3½ ounces pineapple juice

club soda

mango slice, to garnish

freshly ground black
pepper, to garnish

1. Put the gin, rum, brown sugar, lime juice, and pineapple juice into a cocktail shaker.

2. Fill the cocktail shaker with ice cubes and shake until the mixture is well frosted.

3. Strain into an ice cube-filled Collins or highball glass.

4. Top with club soda and garnish with the mango slice and a grinding of black pepper. Serve immediately.

POMEGRANATE & MINT SHRUB

Serves 1

Ingredients

¾ ounce gin

¾ ounce Grand Marnier

sprig of mint, to garnish

1 teaspoon pomegranate
seeds, to garnish

POMEGRANATE SYRUP

1¾ cups pomegranate
seeds

2 cups superfine sugar

20 mint leaves

2 cups raw apple cider
vinegar

1. This cocktail takes two days to steep the syrup. In a medium bowl, muddle the pomegranate seeds, sugar, and mint until the seeds are crushed. Cover and refrigerate to macerate for 24 hours. Remove from the refrigerator and stir in the vinegar. Cover again and refigerate for another 24 hours.

2. Strain the mixture through a piece of cheesecloth. Pour into a sterilized, sealable jar.

3. Fill a highball glass with crushed ice. Add 1¾ ounces of the pomegranate syrup to the glass. The rest can be stored in the refrigerator for up to two months.

4. Add the gin and Grand Marnier to the glass and stir with a bar spoon. Garnish with the mint and pomegranate seeds and serve.

SPICY G&T

Serves 1

Ingredients

1¾ ounces chile-steeped gin

3 splashes molasses bitters

5 ounces tonic water

lime slice, to garnish

CHILE-STEEPED GIN

1 dried pasilla chile

1½ cups gin

1. To make the chile-steeped gin, slice the chile in half lengthwise and put it into the gin bottle. Let steep for one week.

2. To make the cocktail, fill a Collins or highball glass with a handful of ice cubes.

3. Add the gin and molasses bitters and top with tonic water.

4. Garnish with the lime slice and serve immediately.

SPICED WHISKEY SOUR

Serves 1

Ingredients

¾ ounce gin

¾ ounce Pedro Ximénez sherry

¾ ounce bourbon

¾ ounce lemon juice

¾ ounce spiced syrup

1 egg white

SPICED SYRUP

½ cinnamon stick

2 star anise

6 black peppercorns

1⅔ cups superfine sugar

5 ounces water

¾ ounce vodka

1. To make the spiced syrup, gently heat all the ingredients in a medium saucepan over low heat until all the sugar has dissolved.

2. Remove from the heat and let cool, then strain and pour into a bottle. The syrup will keep in the refrigerator for up to six months.

3. To make the cocktail, put the gin, sherry, bourbon, lemon juice, spiced syrup, and egg white into a cocktail shaker. Dry-shake all the ingredients. Add a handful of ice cubes and shake vigorously for 30 seconds to create a foam.

4. Double-strain into an old-fashioned glass and serve immediately.

ROAD RUNNER

Serves 1
Ingredients

1¾ ounces gin

½ ounce dry vermouth

½ ounce Pernod

1 teaspoon grenadine

1. Shake the gin, vermouth, Pernod, and grenadine vigorously over cracked ice until well frosted. Strain into a chilled wine glass and serve immediately.

BELLINI MARTINI

Serves 1
Ingredients

¾ ounce gin

½ ounce brandy

½ ounce peach puree

splash sweet vermouth

peach slice, to garnish

1. Shake the first four ingredients over ice until well frosted. Strain into an iced martini glass and garnish with a slice of peach. Serve immediately.

INCA

Serves 1
Ingredients

¾ ounce gin

¾ ounce sweet vermouth

¾ ounce dry sherry

dash orgeat syrup

dash orange bitters

1. Pour all the ingredients into a glass and stir. This is one that does not need to be chilled. Serve immediately.

BACHELOR'S BAIT

Serves 1
Ingredients

1¾ ounces gin
1 teaspoon grenadine
1 egg white
dash orange bitters

1. Shake the gin, grenadine, and egg white together over ice cubes until well frosted.

2. Add the orange bitters, give the mixture another quick shake, and strain into a chilled cocktail glass. Serve immediately.

OLD
ETONIAN

Serves 1
Ingredients

dash crème de noyaux

dash orange bitters

¾ ounce gin

¾ ounce Lillet blanc

1. Put some cracked ice into a mixing glass and add the liquid ingredients.

2. Stir to mix well, then strain into a chilled cocktail glass. Serve immediately.

MODERN GIN

Over the last decade, gin has risen to become one of the leading liquors in the the United States. Its seemingly unstoppable rise in popularity has been mirrored in the release of hundreds of gin brands and a plethora of specialty bars appearing in cities the world over.

From its somewhat debauched origins in the slums of London, gin has climbed the ladder to reach the peak of sophistication. A true underdog of the liquor world and a classic rags-to-riches tale, this is a feat worthy of recognition. Dozens of factors have combined over the last decade to create this sudden renaissance. Most notably, the micro-distilling boom has led to a fresh wave of artisan distillers creating gins with different flavors, and a soaring global thirst for cocktails has been driven by younger generations looking for drinks with flavor and provenance.

However you choose to buy and drink your gin, you are undoubtedly playing a part in another chapter of gin's history. The gin boom of the early twenty-first century is certainly one that will not be forgotten.

KARINA

Serves 1

Ingredients

¾ ounce gin

½ ounce Dubonnet

½ ounce mandarin liqueur

juice of ½ lemon

1. Mix the ingredients together in a large tumbler filled with ice and stir until the glass is frosted. Serve immediately.

JOCKEY CLUB SPECIAL

Serves 1

Ingredients

¾ ounce gin

½ ounce crème de noyaux

good splash lemon juice

2 dashes orange bitters

2 dashes Angostura bitters

lemon wedge, to garnish

1. Stir the ingredients well over ice and strain into a cocktail glass. Garnish with a lemon wedge. Serve immediately.

ROLLS-ROYCE 2

Serves 1
Ingredients

2½ ounces gin

¾ ounce dry vermouth

¾ ounce sweet vermouth

¼ teaspoon Benedictine

1. Put four to six ice cubes into a mixing glass. Pour the ingredients over the ice. Stir well to mix, then strain into a chilled cocktail glass. Serve immediately.

GREAT DANE

Serves 1

Ingredients

1¾ ounces gin

¾ ounce cherry brandy

½ ounce dry vermouth

1 teaspoon kirsch

lemon peel, to garnish

1. Shake the gin, cherry brandy, vermouth, and kirsch vigorously over ice until well frosted. Strain into a chilled cocktail glass. Garnish with lemon peel. Serve immediately.

STAR
WARS

Serves 1
Ingredients

1¾ ounces gin

1¾ ounces lemon juice

¾ ounce Galliano

¾ ounce crème de noyaux

lemon-peel twist,
to garnish

1. Shake the first four ingredients vigorously over ice until well frosted. Strain into a chilled cocktail glass and garnish with a twist of lemon peel. Serve immediately.

MISSISSIPPI MULE

Serves 1
Ingredients

1¾ ounces gin

½ ounce cassis

½ ounce lemon juice

1. Shake the ingredients vigorously over ice cubes until well frosted. Strain over crushed ice in a small chilled tumbler. Serve immediately.

Chapter 6

---◆---

SPARKLING CUTS

If you like to have a fizz in your tail—or in your cocktail—
look no farther. To make these cocktails effervesce,
we have prosecco, hard cider, soda, and champagne.
Each one is partnered with ingredients in magical
combinations to make sure that your drink, your
companions, and your time together are vibrant
and sparkling.

GIN SWIZZLE

Serves 1

Ingredients

1 cup whiskey-barrel wood chips

1½ cups gin

¾ ounce lime juice

2 teaspoons superfine sugar

1 teaspoon Angostura bitters

6 ounces club soda

lime slice, to garnish

1. This cocktail takes two weeks to steep and you need a chef's blowtorch. Lay the wood chips on a metal tray and put onto a heatproof surface.

2. Scorch the wood chips all over with a blowtorch until about half are blackened. Put the wood chips into a sterilized, sealable jar, then pour in the gin. Keep the gin bottle. Mix and seal the jar. Let steep in a cool place for two weeks.

3. Strain the gin through a fine strainer. Put 1¾ ounces of smoked gin, the lime juice, superfine sugar, and bitters into a highball glass. (The rest of the gin can be stored for up to two months.) Add a large handful of crushed ice to the glass and top with the club soda. Froth well with a swizzle stick and serve immediately with a lime slice.

HONEY & LEMON PROSECCO

Serves 1

Ingredients

¾ ounce gin

¼ ounce honey

¼ ounce lemon juice

3 ounces chilled prosecco

1. Mix the gin, honey, and lemon juice in a small pitcher.

2. Pour the mixture into a chilled coupe glass.

3. Top with the chilled prosecco. Serve immediately.

ELDERFLOWER & MARASCHINO CLUB SODA

Serves 1

Ingredients

¾ ounce gin

¾ ounce elderflower liqueur

¾ ounce maraschino liqueur

½ ounce lemon juice

5 ounces club soda

lemon wedge, to garnish (optional)

maraschino cherry, to garnish

1. Fill a Collins or highball glass with a handful of ice cubes.

2. Add the gin, elderflower liqueur, maraschino liqueur, and lemon juice.

3. Stir the mixture with a cocktail stirrer.

4. Top with the club soda.

5. Garnish with the lemon wedge, if using, and cherry. Serve immediately.

LIME & LEMONGRASS SLING

Serves 1

Ingredients

½ lime

1 small lemongrass stick, trimmed

1¾ ounces gin

½ ounce Benedictine

½ ounce cherry brandy

2 dashes orange bitters

5 ounces club soda

lemon slice and fresh cherry, to garnish

1. Cut the lime into wedges and then slice the lemongrass thinly.

2. Put the lime and lemongrass into a cocktail shaker.

3. Using a muddler, crush the lime and the lemongrass to release the juice and oils.

4. Add the gin, Benedictine, cherry brandy, and orange bitters to the cocktail shaker.

5. Pour the mixture into a sling or highball glass. Add some ice cubes and top with club soda. Garnish with the lemon slice and cherry and serve immediately.

NEW ORLEANS
GIN FIZZ

Serves 1

Ingredients

juice of ½ lemon

2 teaspoons confectioners'
sugar

1 medium egg white

1¾ ounces gin

2 dashes orange flower
water

1 tablespoon light cream

club soda

orange peel and a flower,
to garnish

1. Shake the first six ingredients over ice until well frosted. Strain into a chilled tall tumbler and top with club soda to taste.

2. Garnish with a sliver of orange peel and a flower. Serve immediately.

LONDONER

Serves 1

Ingredients

1¾ ounces London dry gin

½ ounce fraise
(strawberry), rose hip,
or any fruit syrup

1¾ ounces lemon juice

½ ounce dry vermouth

club soda

lemon peel twist,
to garnish

1. Mix the first four ingredients over ice in a highball glass or large tumbler. Top with club soda and garnish with a twist of lemon peel. Serve immediately.

MEDICINAL GIN

Juniperus communis, also known as juniper, is part of the cypress family of plants and is thought to have first appeared during the Triassic period, 250 million years ago. Juniper can be found on almost every continent, weather permitting, and has been used by humankind to treat numerous ailments for thousands of years.

Its medicinal properties were exploited by most ancient civilizations, including those of the Egyptians, Greeks, and Arabs. Its use continued into the Middle Ages, treating everything from toothaches to tapeworms. It was even used as a contraceptive and to induce abortion. Typically, the plant was imbibed in a concoction of wine, spices, and herbs.

No one knows with certainty how juniper first made contact with distilled alcohol, but the earliest references of juniper-flavored liquors date back to the mid-1500s. What we do know is it was the Dutch who created the very first "genevers," the forerunners to English and modern gin. Today, we know that imbibing alcohol and juniper are not conducive to curing illness or preventing pregnancy. However, depending on your circumstances, the ancient healing properties of juniper might make for a reasonable excuse to crack open the gin.

APPLE CLASSIC

Serves 1
Ingredients

½ ounce gin

½ ounce brandy

½ ounce Calvados or other
apple brandy

sweet hard cider

apple slice, to garnish

1. Shake the gin, brandy, and Calvados over ice until frosted.

2. Strain into a glass and top with hard cider to taste.
Garnish with a slice of apple. Serve immediately.

BELLE COLLINS

Serves 1
Ingredients

2 fresh mint sprigs, plus extra
to garnish

1¾ ounces gin

¾ ounce lemon juice

1 teaspoon sugar syrup

sparkling water

1. Muddle the mint sprigs.

2. Put the mint into a chilled tumbler and pour in the gin,
lemon juice, and sugar syrup. Add four to six ice cubes,
crushed, to the glass.

3. Top with sparkling water, stir gently, and garnish with
more fresh mint. Serve immediately.

SOUTHERN FIZZ

Serves 1

Ingredients

1¾ ounces gin

¾ ounce fresh lime juice

¾ ounce passion fruit juice

¼ ounce sugar syrup

3 dashes orange flower water

¾ ounce club soda

1. Mix all the ingredients together with crushed ice in a blender on high for a few seconds, or until really frothy.

2. Pour into a large iced cocktail glass or highball glass and serve immediately.

DAISY

Serves 1
Ingredients

2½ ounces gin

¾ ounce lemon juice

1 tablespoon grenadine

1 teaspoon sugar syrup

club soda

orange wedge, to garnish

1. Put four to six ice cubes, cracked, into a cocktail shaker.

2. Pour the gin, lemon juice, grenadine, and sugar syrup over the ice and shake vigorously until well frosted.

3. Strain the cocktail into a chilled highball glass. Top with club soda, stir gently, and garnish with the orange wedge. Serve immediately.

STAR DAISY

Serves 1
Ingredients

1¾ ounces gin

1¼ ounces apple brandy

1¼ ounces lemon juice

1 teaspoon sugar syrup

½ teaspoon triple sec

club soda

1. Pour the first five ingredients over crushed ice and shake vigorously until well frosted. Strain into a tumbler filled halfway with ice, then top with club soda. Serve immediately.

MONTE CARLO

Serves 1
Ingredients

½ ounce gin

¼ ounce lemon juice

champagne or sparkling
white wine, chilled

¼ ounce crème de menthe

fresh mint sprig, to garnish

1. Put four to six ice cubes, crushed, into a mixing glass and pour the gin and lemon juice over the ice. Stir until well chilled.

2. Strain into a chilled champagne flute and top with champagne.

3. Drizzle the crème de menthe over the top and garnish with the mint sprig. Serve immediately.

SLOE GIN RICKEY

Serves 1
Ingredients

1¾ ounces sloe gin
¾ ounce lime juice
club soda
lime slice

1. Fill a chilled highball glass or goblet with cracked ice.
Pour the gin and lime juice over the ice. Top with club
soda. Stir gently to mix and garnish with a lime slice.
Serve immediately.

END OF THE ROAD

Serves 1

Ingredients

2½ ounces gin

¾ ounce crème de menthe

¾ ounce pastis

3½ ounces club soda

fresh mint sprig,
to garnish

1. Stir the first three ingredients over ice. Strain into a tall glass filled with ice, top with the club soda, and garnish with a sprig of mint. Serve immediately.

ALICE SPRINGS

Serves 1

Ingredients

2½ ounces gin

½ teaspoon grenadine

¾ ounce orange juice

¾ ounce lemon juice

club soda

3 drops Angostura bitters

1. Shake the first four ingredients together over ice until frosted.

2. Strain into a chilled tall glass and top with club soda. Sprinkle in the Angostura bitters.

GIN SANGAREE

Serves 1
Ingredients

1¾ ounces gin

½ teaspoon sugar syrup

sparkling water

1 tablespoon port

freshly grated nutmeg,
for sprinkling

1. Put some cracked ice into a chilled tumbler. Pour the gin and sugar syrup over the ice, then top with sparkling water. Stir gently to mix, then float the port on top.

2. Sprinkle with freshly grated nutmeg and serve immediately.

BLUE BLUE BLUE

Serves 1
Ingredients

¾ ounce gin
¾ ounce vodka
¾ ounce tequila
¾ ounce fresh lemon juice
2 dashes egg white
¾ ounce blue curaçao
club soda
lemon slice, to garnish

1. Put four to six ice cubes, crushed, into a cocktail shaker.

2. Add the gin, vodka, tequila, lemon juice, egg white, and curaçao and shake until frosted.

3. Strain the cocktail into a tall glass filled with crushed ice and top with club soda. Garnish with a lemon slice. Serve immediately.

INDEX

This edition published by Parragon Books Ltd in 2017 and distributed by

Parragon Inc.
440 Park Avenue South, 13th Floor
New York, NY 10016
www.parragon.com/lovefood

LOVE FOOD is an imprint of Parragon Books Ltd

ISBN 978-1-4748-7095-5

Printed in China

Introduction: Joe Clark
New recipes: Lincoln Jefferson
New photography: Mike Cooper
Home economy: Lincoln Jefferson
Cover design: Lexi L'Esteve

Notes for the Reader

This book uses ounces for fluid ounces traditionally measured in a jigger. If you don't have a jigger, a standard jigger = 1½ fluid ounces or 3 tablespoons; 1 tablespoon = ½ fluid ounce. This book also uses standard kitchen measuring spoons and cups. All spoon and cup measurements are level unless otherwise indicated. Unless otherwise stated, milk is assumed to be whole, eggs are large, individual vegetables and fruits are medium, and pepper is freshly ground black pepper.

Please consume alcohol responsibly.